THE YOUNG LAWYER

IN COURT

BY

EARL COX

Edited by

Dean W. Korsak

The Young Lawyer in Court

© 2015 by Dean W. Korsak.

Law Schools and Bar Associations are encouraged to seek permission for use in professional development education programs by emailing dwkorsak@hotmail.com.

Manufactured in the United States of America.
Published by Dandak Publishing, LLC, Mississippi.
Distributed by CreateSpace.com and affiliates.

Paperback:
ISBN-13:   978-0-9814616-6-3
ISBN-10:   0-9814616-6-2

Library of Congress Control Number: 2014958002

Original publication in 1946 by Alpha Publishing
Company, Houston, Texas.

Editor's Preface

H. Earl Cox was a skilled attorney, lecturer, and author.[1] Born in 1900, he passed the Texas Bar Exam twenty-one years later. He attained law firm partner in five years and then hung his own shingle in 1940. He was the president of the Houston Bar Association in 1945 and appointed to the Texas Procedure Rules Body in 1950,[2] the year in which he died.

During his life, Mr. Cox became a significant force within the Texas legal community. His published professional articles include *Errors in Jury Argument*;[3] *The Doctor in Court*,[4] and *Evidence*.[5] In addition to the present book, he authored *A Manual on Jury Argument in Texas Courts*. The Supreme Court of Texas cites him authoritatively numerous times,[6] and he appears as counsel in many reported state and federal cases. All of this leads to the conclusion he was a master

---

[1] 14 Tex. B.J. 44 (1951).
[2] 13 Tex. B.J. 27 (1950).
[3] 6 Tex. B.J. 536 (1943).
[4] 7 Tex. B.J. 141 (1944).
[5] 14 Tex. B.J. 61 (1951).
[6] See e.g. *Southwestern Greyhound Lines v. Dickson*, 236 S.W.2d 115, 119 (1951); *Wade v. Texas Employers' Ins. Ass'n*, 244 S.W.2d 197, 200 (1951).

of his profession. In addition to this mastery, he also cared about how the profession is practiced. This concern led to the writing of the present book.

The book is one of practical experience for those who conduct trials. Upon publication, it was a benefit to both new lawyers and old lawyers who did not frequently engage in trial work. The first publishing took place less than a year after the end of World War Two and was "especially...helpful to veterans whose law practice was interrupted by service in the armed forces."[7] Seven decades later, Earl Cox's advice still inspires young lawyers to master the practice of law.

When a book has an impact on the intended audience there is proven value in the content. The book spoke to an issue of concern in 1946 that still exists today. Lawyers obtain an academic and theoretical education in law school. Upon obtaining a law license, few lawyers are competent to actually orchestrate a trial in court. Experience is sometimes the best teacher, but expert advice and counsel will surely speed the process and reduce the occasion for young lawyers to stumble. Every law graduate should read this book because it will

---

[7] 9 Tex. B.J. 313-314 (1946).

save them "many pitfalls into which…inexperience might otherwise lead…."[8]

The digitizing, editing, annotating and publishing of this work is a tribute to all young lawyers who cut their professional teeth in court. What follows is a polished version of Earl Cox's perspective for modern publication focused on a new generation of attorneys. His timeless counsel is more relevant to modern day trial practice than ever before. Times have changed but the skill set required to gain effectiveness in court has not.

Attorneys inherently struggle with the practical aspects of conducting trials. Earl Cox would tell them today the same thing he advised decades ago. Hone temperament natural to you in court. Have confidence and conviction in your client's cause, your preparation of the case, and your abilities. Respect the Court with your every action. Never underestimate your opponent. Respect the jury. Although many on juries have not had the educational opportunities as you, they have equal or greater intellect and more "horse sense" than many lawyers. Restrain wittiness and attacks to

---

[8] *Id.*

what is useful to your client's cause. That's just the beginning.

Heeding the advice provided in this short book can produce impressive results in court. For example, when a witness is lying on the stand, it is easy to go too far in making a desolate spectacle of the person. The lawyer risks losing credibility and the lying witness can easily gain sympathy. In such situations, Mr. Cox counsels that when the point has been made advantageous to your client's cause, cease speaking and sit down. Continuing the assault for the sake of show hinders the case.

In addition to self-control, skillful lawyers brilliantly lure witnesses to places they do not wish to arrive. This is done with conversational and easy tone, harmless questions about substantive matters that the witness may not know you will later use to your client's advantage. Subtle assaults that are realized in argument long after a cross-examination is complete are much more beneficial than combating witnesses for the sake of producing drama or beating down a conflicting personality. Once skillfully accomplished, the judge, jury, observers, and even opposing counsel will more fully appreciate your client's cause. This is a great achievement for any lawyer in court and is attainable in nearly every case.

All lawyers have a war chest full of stories. It is with sincere hope that this book will provide lawyers with opportunities to create more positive stories with results to back them up. To this end, the editing of Earl Cox's words focused on modernizing the text to convey the essence of the advice by smoothing the edges off of some antiquated phrases and concepts that would hinder the message. Care was taken to preserve much of the original formatting, words, phrases, and perspectives that are not overly distractive. What follows below is a format and text that will speak to lawyers young and old for many more decades to come. May it bring the reader the best results in court and inspire many to further the professional practice of our ancient profession.

Sincerely,

Dean Korsak

This is the highest quality photo available of Earl Cox, digitized from the photo located at 14 Tex. B.J. 61 (February 1951).

The Texas Bar Journal Archives is due credit for verifying the original photograph is not in the archives.

THE YOUNG LAWYER

IN COURT

BY

EARL COX

Houston, Texas, 1946

Alpha Publishing Company
Houston, Texas

TO MY FRIEND

ALLEN B. HANNAY[9]

---

[9] Allen Burroughs Hannay was born in 1892. In 1913 he graduated from the University of Texas School of Law. He practiced law in Hempstead, Texas and served as a Texas state court judge until 1942. In that year, Franklin D. Roosevelt nominated him, the Senate confirmed him, and he was commissioned a federal district court judge for the Southern District of Texas. He served as chief judge from 1954-1962 and assumed senior status in 1975 until his death in 1983. See Biographical Directory of Federal Judges, available at http://www.fjc.gov.

INTRODUCTION

Young lawyers first beginning to practice, even though they are well trained in the law, usually find when they begin the trial of lawsuits that there are many things about court room procedure that are a closed book to them. Particularly is this true of matters of personal conduct and the tactics to be pursued in given situations. They will have found little in their law books to help them in their dealings with other lawyers and with judges, jurors and witnesses. It is with the hope of assisting the beginner in these incidental matters pertaining to trial work that this little book is written.

Just as the doctor must acquire a fitting "bedside manner" as a necessary adjunct to the successful practice of that profession, the lawyer who seeks success in the trial of lawsuits must acquire an appropriate court room presence. While experience is the best teacher in this regard, it is thought that some words of advice may be of help.

The suggestions and observations made herein are based upon ideas acquired and experiences had during the trial of cases for a quarter of a century. The writer claims no literary ability, and if his ideas as to the manner in which the lawyer should conduct himself in court do not appear sound in all particulars, he can only say that they are his own ideas based upon his own experience and observation.

EARL COX

Houston, Texas,
November 1st, 1945

CONTENTS

1. YOU

You have now become a lawyer and are ready to begin the practice of your profession. By hard work and application you have fitted yourself for your life's work from the academic standpoint. However, you are somewhat in the position of a workman who is possessed of a fine set of carpenter's tools but has had no experience in the erection of a house. In such a case advice from one who had erected many houses would be of benefit. In your case advice with reference to the practical aspects of the practice of your profession, and in particular the trial of lawsuits, should be of help to you in the use of the tools which you have acquired.

Your profession is an ancient and honorable one and one in which you should take great pride. In the present day it is quite the thing to speak disparagingly of lawyers. In motion pictures and the comic strips they are usually depicted as being tricky and dishonest, if not out and out villains. This attitude is assumed by some persons who should know better. Owen P. White in his autobiography which was published a short time ago says that, in comparing members of the legal profession to the hated sect of Pharisees, Christ said, "Woe to you lawyers, because you load people with burdens very hard to carry and you will not lift a finger to help them," and further states that "the President of the Association of the Bar of New York bluntly affirmed that 'two-thirds of all American lawyers have not the slightest interest in the science of jurisprudence, or in the good name, honor and dignity of the profession.'"[10] In your professional life you should ever be on the alert to combat this attitude. You can do your part by conducting your own professional career in a manner above reproach, and by being outspoken in defense of your profession whenever ill is spoken of it.

You should always bear in mind that you are a lawyer and not a tradesman; that the achievement of as high a place in your profession as your capacities will permit is your goal, and not the

---

[10] Owen P. White, "The Autobiography of a Durable Sinner." By permission of G. P. Putnam's Sons, publishers.

mere acquisition of money. In ancient Greece and later in Rome the lawyers received no fees, but sometimes accepted gratuities. They were not practicing law for financial gain. The idea of making money out of the practice of law is comparatively modern. Even as late as the Eighteenth Century young people contemplating a legal career were admonished that they should not undertake such a course unless they were financially independent; for if they were dependent for their livelihood upon fees realized from the practice of law they might be tempted to resort to practices incompatible with the high ideals that a lawyer should have. These old ideas are too extreme for our modern day world, for we must have many lawyers, and most of them must support themselves by their practice. Nevertheless, you must always bear in mind that the practice of your profession is different from the conducting of a trade or business. You are a fiduciary, occupying a position of trust and confidence. Your service is as personal as that of a physician. It cannot be brought down to the level of a mere business transaction. The practice of the law itself and your advancement in the profession should be to you the matter of primary importance, and the making of money only secondary.

You probably wish to be a trial lawyer. Almost every young lawyer beginning the practice believes that to be a real lawyer one must try lawsuits. It is only later that he finds that "many are called but few are chosen," and somewhat later still discovers that this is not such a bad situation after all; that office practice is much easier on the nerves and oftentimes more desirable. But, assuming that you wish to try cases, we will proceed from that point.

At the very beginning you must realize that there is no standard type of trial lawyer. People of absolutely divergent characteristics may be equally adept and successful in the court room. A lawyer may be tall or short, handsome or homely, aggressive to the point of belligerency or mild to the point of timidity, and still be a successful trial lawyer. It is purely a matter of work and application; the taking advantage of every favorable element in your physical and mental makeup, and being yourself under any and all circumstances. Just be your natural self, whatever your temperament may be, for if you attempt to be something other than you are you succeed in being nothing.

The matter of personal appearance, so far as physical characteristics are concerned, does not play a large part in the winning or losing of lawsuits, although the lawyer's demeanor, as is hereinafter pointed out, can be of controlling importance. The question of dress is also not a matter of great moment. One very successful trial lawyer who represented railroad companies in Texas Courts for many years dressed shabbily, never wore a necktie, and during the trial of a case never shaved. On one occasion, after having won a verdict from a jury in a Federal Court, the jurors took up a collection among themselves and presented the lawyer with the price of a shave. He was not at all disconcerted, but was quite pleased. He had won his case, which was the main thing. Going to the other extreme, the famed California criminal lawyer, Earl Rogers, always wore a cutaway coat, striped trousers and spats in court, and the late Samuel Untermyer, a great trial lawyer of New York City, wore an orchid in his buttonhole when trying a case, and changed it constantly for fresh ones brought to him from his office throughout the trial. Each of these lawyers dressed according to his own lights and they were equally successful. They were being themselves. Some lawyers believe that they should "dress down" for the jury; that they should try to make their appearance similar to that of most jurors. This is not necessary, for ordinarily jurors do not expect a lawyer to be as they are, but expect something different; otherwise why should he be the lawyer and they the jurors?

As before indicated, while the trial lawyer's personal appearance, either from the physical standpoint or the standpoint of dress, is not of great importance, his demeanor in the court room can constitute the difference between success and failure. When you go into the trial of a lawsuit you occupy, more or less, the position of a salesman attempting to sell a bill of goods. You are trying to convince the jury of the correctness of your contentions. To do this you must be absolutely sincere. Whether in fact you are right or wrong you must yourself believe that you are right. If you can't believe that you are right you cannot be sincere. If you are not being your natural self you cannot be sincere. If you are not sincere you will seldom prevail, for in spite of all of the things that are said of jurors, they can usually detect insincerity instantly, and hard is your lot when the jury gets the impression that you do not yourself completely believe the contentions you are urging. First and foremost, be utterly sincere at all times when trying a lawsuit. Be yourself all of the time, for being your natural self is the first and most important step in being sincere. If you are the aggressive type, be aggressive. If you are the mild type then be mild and do not attempt to assume an aggressiveness that is not natural to you. You must exhibit in the court room that demeanor which is suited to your temperament, for you cannot convincingly assume another. If you are not naturally aggressive do not attempt the aggressive approach, for you will strike a false note. You will give the impression of not being sincere. If you are one of those fortunate mortals who is possessed of real wit and humor then permit yourself to be witty upon occasion, but be careful not to overdo it. If you are not naturally humorous, never attempt humor in the courtroom; for nothing can fall so flat and make one feel so cheap as a bright remark met by a stony faced stare from the jury.

While your natural temperament cannot be changed (it is said that temperament is fixed and determined by the time a person is three years of age) and you must, in the fundamental particulars, suit your demeanor to your temperament in order to achieve that sincerity that is the most important prerequisite of the trial lawyer, yet there are some essential rules of conduct in the court room that you should religiously observe, even though they be contrary to your nature, and which can be observed without loss of sincerity on your part.

You should be unfailingly courteous at all times; courteous to the trial judge, to the witnesses, to your opponent and to all others with whom you come into contact in the court room. You should conduct yourself with dignity at all times. Unless you are a natural humorist you should be grave and serious. Humor is a dangerous thing. You should not attempt it unless you are an expert at it. Ordinarily it is safer to treat your case as a serious undertaking and approach it with seriousness and gravity. Except in unusual circumstances levity is out of place in the courtroom. You should exercise self-control at all times. Do not permit yourself to lose your temper under any circumstances. Practice control of your facial expression so that you do not involuntarily reveal that your side of the case has been injured by some ruling of the court or answer of a witness. Do not gloat or show undue elation over some favorable occurrence during the trial for matters may take a different turn shortly thereafter resulting in your own discomfiture. Do not attempt familiarity with the jurors, either during the trial or at recess; preserve a respectful but somewhat aloof attitude toward them. In fine, try and conduct yourself at all times during the trial in a dignified, respectful, courteous and equable manner.

From the very beginning of your career try to develop a courtroom personality that is your own. Do not attempt to pattern yourself after other lawyers. All people are different. There are no two exactly alike. There may be trial lawyers for whom you have admiration and you may wish to be like them. Except superficially this cannot be done. You must be yourself, for you can't be someone else. School yourself to the end that you may secure full advantage of your own natural endowments and then –be yourself.

2. YOUR OPPONENT

In the practice of your profession you will encounter all types of lawyers. Now and then you will encounter one who is profound; usually they will be run of the mill lawyers, and sometimes below average. In any event do not be critical but endeavor to be friendly with all of them. Make no enemies among the members of the bar if you can possibly avoid it, for the friendship and respect of your fellow lawyers is essential to real success in your profession.

When you begin the practice of law you will discover to your surprise that some lawyers that you encounter who have been practicing for many years are not proficient – to put it mildly. Such experiences have the tendency to make you feel superior. However, the longer you practice the more tolerant you will become for you will find that while perhaps a certain lawyer is totally inexperienced in the line of practice in which you are proficient, he may be adept in another type of endeavor of which you know nothing.

Do not judge your fellow lawyers, but be friendly and courteous, and if the occasion demands, charitable towards them all.

In the preparation and trial of a lawsuit do not underrate your opponent. It is wise to always proceed on the assumption that your adversary is as proficient as you are and has worked as hard on his case. If you will follow this course you will seldom encounter unpleasant surprises. On the other hand do not overrate your opponent, for no matter what his standing may be in the profession he is just another lawyer in the courtroom, and if you have a meritorious case and have left no stone unturned in preparing it for trial, you have nothing to fear. Few cases are won on personality; many, if not all, are won on painstaking preparation. The law is in the books and the facts are in the testimony. If you have completely prepared yourself on the law and the facts, and if your cause is a just one, you will prevail whatever the caliber of your opponent.

In the trial of a case always treat the opposing attorney with extreme courtesy. In addition to being the pleasant and gracious thing to do, such conduct makes a good impression upon the jury. Do not permit yourself to be drawn into extraneous argument in the presence of the jury. Avoid, as far as possible, addressing the opposing lawyer during the trial. Direct your remarks to the Court. There is little to be said between attorneys while trying a lawsuit, and unnecessary conversations sometimes lead to unpleasant occurrences. The lawyers on both sides are under tension; they are engaged in a battle, and the less they say to one another the better. If your opponent resorts to side-bar remarks, as often happens, do not reply in kind, but address yourself to the Court in seeking relief.

Avoid as much as possible argumentative discourse with your opponent, either before or during the trial, with reference to the merits of the controversy which is being litigated. Do not boast about your certainty of winning the lawsuit. If your opponent takes such attitude, do not reply in kind. Such boastful conduct is rather common among young lawyers. Usually it is but an unconscious effort on their part to cover up their feeling of uncertainty. Such course should be avoided, for once you begin an argument with your opponent about the merits of your case and the possible outcome thereof, you usually find yourself forced, in self-defense and possibly against your will, to make more extravagant claims and assertions than are justified. You are compelled to take a position that is immodest, to say the least, and one that may be distasteful to you. Furthermore, in the heat of the moment you may reveal matters and things about your side of the case that may forewarn your opponent. While you should never reveal any lack of confidence in your cause it is always better to avoid predicting its outcome or bragging about what you are going to do.

Be a good winner as well as a good loser. Never exult over your victories, for the shoe may be on the other foot the next time you try a case with your opponent. If you lose your case take your loss with good grace and congratulate your opponent. If you have preserved a modest attitude throughout in your dealings with your opponent, as suggested in the last paragraph, you will not feel your loss so keenly and your opponent will be deprived of some of the pleasures of victory.

Of course, it goes without saying, that you must never resort to "sharp" practices, or in any way mistreat your adversary. If you are mistreated, as you probably will be from time to time, do not attempt to retaliate. Make a practice of overlooking the slights and unfair tactics that you may encounter from other lawyers. Do not bear a grudge or become unfriendly. If you were only going to experience one episode in your career in which you thought you were mistreated, it would not be so bad to break off friendly relations with the lawyer involved. However, you are going to practice law for a long time, and if you become an enemy to every lawyer that you believe has wronged you during your professional career, you may end up by finding that you have more enemies than friends. It is better to forget such unpleasant occurrences, for nothing can be gained by falling out with your opponent, or attempting to "get even."

Seek at all times to gain the good will and respect of your fellow lawyers. Make no enemies among them if it is at all possible to avoid it. One enemy can do your career more harm than ten friends can benefit it, for your enemy will certainly work at the matter and your friends may not.

3. THE TRIAL JUDGE

If you are to try lawsuits in court you must gain the respect and confidence of the Judges before whom you appear. To do this you must exhibit at all times proper respect for the Judge and must be absolutely fair and honest with him.

If the Judge respects your ability and has confidence in your integrity his attitude toward you is calculated to be such as that the jury is made aware of such fact and they, in turn, may acquire the same feeling. On the other hand, if your conduct is such as to cause the Judge to feel otherwise, such feeling is quickly communicated to the jury. It is imperative that you remain in the good graces of the "Court."

Judges are but human, with the same differences and peculiarities as other people. The respect that you must have and exhibit at all times is not for the person but for the office the person occupies. Even though you may not think much of the person you must respect the office.

By and large, judges attempt to be fair and impartial. Usually they are impartial. If the Judge rules against you do not feel that he does so because of bias or prejudice. Bear in mind that while the case you are trying may mean a great deal to you, it is just another case to him; perhaps one of many hundreds that he disposes of throughout the year. Once in a great while you may encounter a prejudiced judge or one who is tyrannical. In such instances you may on occasion experience a difficult time. When confronted with such a situation the best course to pursue is to maintain a tight rein upon your emotions and try and preserve your equanimity. You must not lose your temper, for you will make conditions worse. You should be even more punctilious in your conduct and in your respectful attitude toward the Court than usual. Such an attitude may prove helpful. At all events no other course that you may take can be of benefit to you, for if you show impatience or become rude you will probably antagonize the Judge and make your situation worse. Always bear in mind that in the trial of a lawsuit you are in many cases at the mercy the Judge. No matter what your personal feelings may be, it is your duty to your client's cause to try and get along with the Judge under any and all circumstances.

You should be careful of your conduct in the court room to the end that your attitude, words and actions may at all times evidence proper respect for the Court. It should be your effort throughout your career to preserve the dignity of the court room. In the trial of a case you should always address the Judge in such terms as "Your Honor" or "if Your Honor please," and when addressing him you should always rise to your feet. You should not sprawl in your chair, elevate your feet or sit upon the counsel table. It is well to observe these rules at the very beginning of your career and in any and all courts, no matter how inferior, that you may find yourself, for by so doing such conduct upon your part will develop into such a fixed habit and custom that you will never have to give the matter further thought but will always act in a manner becoming to the dignity of any court room in which you may appear.

Always be absolutely honest with the trial Judge. Never make a statement to him that the decisions hold thus and so on a proposition of law unless you know for a certainty that such is the case. Many lawyers, to win a point, will state to the Judge that the decisions hold a certain thing to be the law, when they do not know whether or not such is the case, and sometimes when they know that the decisions hold otherwise. You should never indulge in such practice, for if the Judge finds that you have knowingly or carelessly misrepresented the law to him he may lose all confidence in you and you will thereafter have a difficult time convincing him, even when you are right. If you will follow the policy of never making an outright assertion to a Judge that the law is a certain way unless you know that you are absolutely correct, and unless you are prepared to back your statement up with authority, you will gradually win the confidence of the Judges before whom you appear and will find that in time those who get to know you well will be inclined to accept your statement as to what the law is; sometimes without the necessity of your producing supporting authority.

In arguing law questions to the trial Judge you should be absolutely fair. Never attempt to present a decision as the law when you know that it has been overruled and is no longer authority. Do not read to the Court only that part of a decision that is favorable to you and omit a part that may be hurtful. Do not in any manner attempt to mislead the Court. Discuss the cases that hold against your contentions as well as those that are in your favor and then seek to differentiate them. There is no use in attempting to ignore the unfavorable decisions; your opponent will bring them to the attention of the Court. You may as well meet the situation head-on in the first instance and discuss your opponent's decisions as well as your own. By so exhibiting to the Court your familiarity with the decisions on both sides of your question and the fact that you do not fear bringing the unfavorable decisions to the attention of the Court, you are likely to be placed in a more favorable position with the Court than you would be if you ignored the decisions of your opponent and permitted him to present them to the Court as a matter of first impression.

When you do not know what the law is on a certain question never fail to admit such fact to the Judge. If the Judge propounds a question of law to you and you do not know the answer, frankly admit your lack of knowledge. In such a case you may voice your opinion on the subject, but state it as an opinion, or the hazarding of a guess, and not as a fact. Tell the Court "I do not know the law on that question, but I will examine the decisions." Then examine the decisions before you take a stand. Never pretend a knowledge that you do not possess, for while you may get by in a few instances, if such course is pursued you will find that you have done yourself more harm than good.

In the trial of a case seldom argue with the Judge about his rulings. Ordinarily such argument does no good and tends to antagonize him. If the Judge overrules your objections to the evidence or sustains the objections of the other side, never argue with him unless you know that you are absolutely right and can at that very time produce authority for your position. Unless you can sustain your position with authority at the very time of the ruling, you are wasting time arguing with the Judge about his position, for the more you argue the more positive in his opinion he is likely to become. Ordinarily such argument, unsupported by authority, is fruitless; it is a waste of time, and if made in the presence of the jury may be injurious to your cause.

As stated before you must keep in the good graces of the Court. To be successful as a trial lawyer you must have the confidence and respect of the Court. If you will, throughout your career, adopt and follow such a course as is here suggested you should gain the respect and confidence of the Judges before whom you appear, and in time you will find that the esteem in which you are held by the Judges in whose courts you practice creates an atmosphere in the courtroom that is most helpful to you before the jury.

4. THE JURY

You are now proceeding to the trial of your case. We will assume that it is to be a jury trial. Of course, you wish to get on your jury persons who are as favorable as possible to your side of the controversy, and you wish to eliminate therefrom persons that you think may be unfavorable.

If you are in a Court that permits direct questioning of the jury panel by the attorneys, and most of them do, you should begin the trying of your case with the very first statement that you make to the prospective jurors. In the very beginning, and before starting your interrogation, tell the jury panel what the case is about and what your contentions are, being careful to frame your statement in as favorable a light to your side of the case as the proprieties will permit. Your attitude should be one of dignified seriousness. Attempt to impress the jurors at the outset with the fact that they are about to embark upon a serious undertaking. There is little place for frivolity or levity on such an occasion.

If you do not treat your case as a serious matter you cannot expect the jury to consider it in a serious light. In addressing the jury panel be careful to speak in a tone sufficiently loud so that no one on the panel will have difficulty in hearing and understanding you.

Ordinarily there is no necessity for lengthy questioning of the individual juror. Particularly is this true in a civil suit. If you ascertain the names of the prospective jurors, their residences, their present and past occupations, their marital status, and whether or not they know any of the litigants or attorneys, or anything about the pending litigation, you have secured about all the information obtainable that can be of assistance to you in determining which of the jurors you wish to strike from the jury list. Many lawyers consume a great deal of time in asking prospective jurors useless questions. There is little to be gained in asking a prospective juror whether he has any feeling of prejudice or bias in one respect or another. If he is prejudiced or biased he probably does not know it, and if he is aware of such fact will probably not admit it.

To determine prejudice or bias you must look to the person's background and decide in your own mind whether or not such emotional phenomenon is apt to exist. After all, the selection of a jury is largely a guess and a gamble, and after ascertaining the background of the prospective jurors you will have to rely to a great extent on such intuition as you may possess.

The greatest benefit to be derived from your interrogation of the jury panel lies not so much in what the prospective jurors tell you about themselves, but in the opportunity that is afforded you to get acquainted with them and to be able to carefully look each of them over; to note their facial expressions, their physical peculiarities and their apparent reaction to you as an individual. You should attempt to strike from the jury list those jurors with whom you feel no compatibility of spirit; those people whom you instinctively feel would not be inclined to follow your ideas; in other words, those of the jurors whom you believe do not "like" you and that you do not "like."

You know from your experience in the ordinary walks of life that you meet people every day that you instinctively like or dislike. You may rest assured that ordinarily when you encounter a person that you dislike on first meeting, this feeling is mutual. For some psychological reason not as yet fully explained by our community of science certain people have a marked antipathy for one another. It is something of an intangible nature that one immediately senses and feels. In the number of prospective jurors appearing on the panel there will usually be some people who are your "opposites" in the sense here suggested. You should eliminate these people from the jury which is to try your case. When examining the jury panel, and as you come to each juror, ask yourself "is this a man that I can talk to; is he a man that will follow my ideas; is he a man that I would like and who would like me," and attempt, as far as possible, to get on your jury jurors who fall within this category. In dealing with such intangibles as are here mentioned the manner in which the prospective juror answers your questions, together with his appearance and demeanor, is usually far more important than the answers which they give to the questions which you propound.

Leaving aside the rather abstruse features of jury selection last mentioned, there are some broad, time-tested principles governing the matter that should be borne in mind. A juror's predilections are created and produced by the position which he occupies in society and by his own personal experiences in life. The man of property is usually conservative; the poor man liberal. A jury of common workers can usually be depended upon to find in favor of persons of the working class and of those with lower income in society as against a corporation or a person of wealth. The rich person, the executive, the person of property will usually find for the corporate interests or persons of property. As Arthur Train has well said "The rich man is apt to think more highly of the institutions which protect his riches than the poor man, who has none and who may suspect that the system isn't all that it is cracked up to be."[11] While this is perhaps not a desirable situation, it exists and the lawyer is justified in taking advantage of it. It is the instinct of the person of property to protect property rights. He is therefore a poor juror for the claimant in any type of suit seeking the recovery of

---

[11] The American Magazine, November, 1924, page 148. Dwight G. McCarty "Psychology for the Lawyer," By permission of Prentice-Hall, Inc., publishers, and the American Magazine.

damages, but is an excellent juror for the litigant seeking to avoid the payment of such damages. On the other hand the poor person, or the average worker, has little sympathy with property rights, and is usually quite willing to award liberal damages; particularly against corporations or persons of wealth. Young people are usually liberal, whereas older people tend to be conservative. People with a highly emotional temperament are ordinarily very sympathetic and liberal and make good plaintiffs' jurors. Jurors who are engaged in the same occupation as a litigant, or who are of the same background, or occupy the same position in society, are inclined to favor that litigant.

When representing a claimant in any type of action for damages, or when representing a working man or a person without means in any kind of litigation, you should endeavor to get common workers and people without means on your jury. When representing a corporation, or a person known to the jury to be wealthy, or when defending any type of action for damages, you should try and get on your jury as many business people, executives and those of wealth and property as you possibly can.

A few actual occurrences illustrating the varying attitudes of men from different walks of life who sit on juries may well be set forth here. In one case, a personal injury action, the jury returned a verdict in the sum of $27,000.00 in favor of an elderly housewife of no earning capacity who had suffered a broken leg. The verdict was grossly excessive under the facts in the case. When asked why he had agreed upon such a verdict one of the jurors, a barber by trade, replied, "I was holding out for an award of $40,000.00. This was the first time I ever had the opportunity of dealing with big money and I wanted to be liberal." This man was determined to be "liberal" with money belonging to someone else without regard to the facts in the case. In another instance a lawyer who was attending a social gathering met a friend of his who was a minor executive with a large public utility company. In the ensuing conversation the lawyer mentioned to his friend the fact that he was going to trial shortly in a case in which he represented a man who had lost an arm when the motor bus in which he was riding as a passenger came into collision with another automobile. Without being told anything whatsoever about the facts in the case the executive stated "Well, if I was on the jury you would have to prove to my satisfaction that the bus company was at fault before I would give your client any damages." Even though he knew nothing of the facts in the case this man instantly decided the case in his own mind adversely to the claimant. In another case that was tried, being an action against a trucking concern for the recovery of damages because of personal injuries, two of the jurors hung the jury for twenty-four hours in favor of the trucking company. These two men were themselves in the trucking business, one as a driver and the other as an office worker. The mere fact that they were engaged in the same line of endeavor as was the defendant in the cause was sufficient to cause them to see the case in a light favorable to such defendant.

It must be understood that jurors are not consciously unfair. They usually believe that they are deciding a case on the evidence introduced upon the trial, and would be greatly hurt if told that their decision had really been based upon sympathy, bias, prejudice or some other emotional phenomena. However, the fact remains that jurors are governed in their decisions far more by their emotions than they are by their reasoning powers. It is a matter of the workings of the subconscious mind. Almost always those sitting on a jury attempt to be fair and honest in their decisions and to do what they consider to be the right thing. However, the "right thing" according to the conception of the jury is not always the fair or proper thing when considered from the standpoint of the cold logic of the law.

After all is said and done, the fact remains that in the selection of jurors you are taking a gamble and there is never any certainty as to what a jury will do. It is possible that all of the worry and thought that goes into the selection of a jury; the painful effort incident to arriving at a decision as to whether to take this person or eliminate that person, is a waste of time. At all events, one great trial lawyer, Henry A. Uterhart, has arrived at that decision. He says, "I have come to the conclusion that the first twelve [people] that are put in the box are just about as good as any twelve jurors you might select. In the first Creasy murder trial I spent four days in selecting a jury and they convicted him of murder in the first degree in less than an hour, without looking at one of the hundreds of exhibits which had been placed in evidence and upon which the whole defense depended. In the second trial I took the first twelve [people] that came in the box and acquitted him. 'So, uncle, there you are,' as Hamlet said."[12]

All you can do in selecting your jury is to try and observe a few simple rules, such as those mentioned above, rely upon such intuition as you may have, and trust to luck.

---

[12] Frances L. Wellman, "Success in Court." By permission of The McMillan Company, publishers.

5. THE WITNESS

The witnesses are now being placed upon the stand; your witnesses by whom you expect to prove your case and the witnesses of the opposition whose testimony you must mitigate to as great an extent as possible.

Ordinarily witnesses in a lawsuit, no matter how truthful and honest they may be, tend to take sides; to identify themselves with the side that places them upon the witness stand, and this tendency sometimes causes a witness to go farther in his testimony and to testify more strongly for the side that places him on the stand than the facts warrant. Especially is this true where the witness is severely pressed on cross-examination. This peculiarity of witnesses is made apparent to an observer in almost any case that is tried. During interrogation on direct examination by the attorney who has placed him upon the witness stand, the attitude of the witness will usually be observed to be one of helpful cooperation. However, when the direct examination ceases and cross-examination is begun by the lawyer for the opposing side, a distinct change in attitude can usually be observed upon the part of the witness. He squares himself in the witness chair, becomes careful and alert and by his every act and word indicates that he is on his guard; which in fact he is. He usually feels that he has told his story, and that it is true, and that any questioning by the other side is in effect an attack upon his credibility. While actual hostility to the cross-examiner is seldom shown, usually it exists to some degree. While, by and large, most witnesses are honest and are attempting to tell the truth, the fact remains that, even though subconsciously, they are inclined to favor the side that has called them as witnesses, and to look with disfavor, if not actual hostility, upon the litigants and their attorneys who are on the opposite side of the case. Thus, to some extent at least, the lawyer trying a lawsuit is justified in feeling that the witnesses placed on the stand by him are attempting to assist his cause by their testimony, and that the witnesses of his adversary are bent upon rendering all the assistance they can to the other side – in other words, he is justified in feeling that the witnesses are not wholly disinterested people. Accordingly, the trial lawyer in conducting the trial should perform his functions, within the bounds of propriety of course, as if the witnesses placed upon the stand by him were active aides in behalf of his cause, and as if the witnesses of the opposition were his adversaries.

We will first consider the witnesses placed on the stand by you in support of your case. It goes without saying that you should first go over the witness' testimony with him before he takes the witness stand. You should not place a witness on the stand unless you know exactly what his testimony will be. In discussing the witness' testimony with him you should not only ascertain from him just what his answers will be to the questions you propose propounding to him, but should also determine just what his answers will be to the questions which your opponent may ask him on cross-examination. You should instruct the witness to tell the whole truth in connection with anything about which he is interrogated; that while he should not volunteer any information, he should answer truthfully any question that is asked him.

It is well to confer with each witness separately and privately. While there is nothing unethical about conferring with witnesses as a group, still if such fact is brought out on cross-examination by the other side it may prove hurtful. Your opponent may then argue that you and the witnesses got together and "rehearsed" the testimony; that the witnesses had been taken to "witness school;" that the purpose of conferring with them in a group was to "iron out" or reconcile differences in their testimony.

You should instruct each of your witnesses before he takes the stand that if he is asked whether he has discussed the case or his testimony with anyone that he should answer truthfully and state when and with whom he discussed such matters. When witnesses are sworn and placed under the rule they are instructed by the Court not to discuss the case with anyone. They often confuse the meaning of this instruction, and when they are placed on the stand and the lawyer for the opposition takes them on cross-examination and asks them if they have ever discussed the case or their proposed testimony with anyone, they feel that to admit such a discussion would reveal that they had violated the rules of the court, and many times will deny the fact. It is quite surprising how often this occurs. Of course, the jury knows that the witness must have discussed the case with the attorney placing him on the stand, or else the lawyer would not have known what the witness' testimony would be, and consequently the jury knows that the witness is not telling the truth when he denies such discussion. Every witness placed on the stand should be warned in the manner above mentioned. To illustrate how embarrassing such a denial of a minor fact can become it may be mentioned that some lawyers will ask a witness on cross-examination if he has ever discussed the facts in the case with anyone, including the lawyer on the other side, and if the witness denies such discussion, the examiner will call the opposing attorney to the stand as a witness and prove by him that such discussion actually took place. This will only have to happen to you once to cause you to make it an invariable rule to instruct your witnesses to answer truthfully when asked whether they have discussed the case with you.

You should instruct your witnesses to speak in a clear voice and in a voice loud enough to be heard at all times. The witness should be instructed not to smoke or to chew gum while on the witness stand. He should be instructed not to place his hand over his mouth while testifying. Many witnesses – in fact a great many – unless warned in advance will place their hands or fingers over their mouths while testifying. This is ordinarily caused by nothing more than nervousness or a want of ease. However, it is generally supposed that such a gesture indicates that the witness is not telling the truth, and out of the twelve people on the jury some of them may entertain this idea. At all events, such action on the part of the witness tends to make it difficult for the jury to hear and understand him and, if for no other reason, should be avoided. The witness should be instructed to look at his questioner when being interrogated, and should be told not to look at the attorney who placed him on the stand when being cross-examined by the lawyer for the other side. A witness being subjected to cross-examination makes a poor impression on the jury when he turns his gaze to the lawyer who placed him upon the stand, for the impression is created that he is seeking assistance or "coaching" in his testimony. Some lawyers will have the witness turn to the jury when testifying to certain matters, saying "now please turn around and face the jury and tell them just what occurred." This is done for the purpose of having the witness look into the eyes of the jury while telling his story and thus convince them by his appearance and attitude that he is telling the truth. This practice may be all right in some cases and with certain witnesses, but it is not to be recommended, for usually it fails of its purpose. The witness is ill at ease enough because of the mere fact that he is on the witness stand, and when he is asked to turn to the jury and tell his story he is still more embarrassed and ordinarily his testimony takes on an artificial and unconvincing air. For such a course of procedure to produce desirable results the witness must be one with some histrionic ability. In most cases the testimony will be more convincing if the witness addresses himself to his interrogator.

When representing the plaintiff in cases being defended by an undisclosed insurance company, all of the witnesses should be warned in advance not to mention the word "insurance" or "insurance adjuster" while testifying on the stand, for in most jurisdictions the injecting into the case of any testimony whatsoever that tends to reveal the fact, otherwise unknown to the jury, that an insurance company is defending the action will result in a mistrial. In this type of case it is well not only to warn your own witnesses in this regard, but to have opposing counsel or the Court also warn the witnesses on the other side. It is most disappointing to be in the trial of a case for a number of days and have everything going well, and then to have a mistrial declared merely because a witness inadvertently mentions the word "insurance."

You should always "invoke the rule" before the testimony is begun. By "placing the witnesses under the rule" is meant the action of the Court in excluding all witnesses, except parties to the cause, from the courtroom during the progress of the trial, and instructing them not to discuss the case among themselves or permit anyone to discuss it with them except the lawyers participating in the trial. By this method no witness, except a party to the suit, is permitted to hear the testimony of any other witness. The invocation of the rule prevents the witnesses of your adversary from hearing the testimony of your witnesses and the testimony of each other and changing, conforming or reconciling their testimony. It is a very salutary rule and one that will often prove helpful to you when cross- examining the witnesses of your adversary, as will be hereinafter pointed out.

You have now placed your witness on the stand and your direct examination is in progress. Make it a rule to always speak in a clear voice loud enough to be heard by everyone concerned. Start your examination of the witness rather slowly and in a gentle and reassuring manner. Give the witness time to collect his faculties and become adjusted to his surroundings. Carry the witness along through the preliminary and relatively unimportant features of his testimony until you are certain that he is over his first nervousness and is at ease, and then proceed with the material aspects of your interrogation. This allowance of a period of adjustment for the witness is quite important, for most witnesses are so ill at ease when they take the witness stand that it is difficult for them to concentrate. You, yourself, will find that this is true if you are ever placed on the witness stand. No matter how many years you practice and try lawsuits in the courts you will find that when your role is reversed and you become the witness you, too, will suffer from "stage fright." Incidentally it is a known fact that most lawyers make very poor witnesses. Strange to say, the more ignorant a witness may be the less nervous and ill at ease he is on the witness stand. This is probably due to lack of imagination. On the other hand the more intelligent and high-strung a person is the more difficult it is for him to become adjusted to the unaccustomed atmosphere of the witness box. The course to follow should be regulated in accordance with the temperament of each witness.

In the developing of your case by your witnesses on direct examination you should consume only the time necessary to get all of your facts before the jury. Your questions should be framed in such manner as to be unobjectionable from a legal standpoint and as to be clear and concise enough to be instantly understood by the witness and to elicit from him the answers desired. No aimless or unnecessary questions should be asked. Give thought to each question as you propound it to make certain that it is clear and easily understood. Take your time in this regard. Think before you speak. Formulate each question in your mind before it is asked. If the testimony is of a type difficult of elicitation it is well to write your questions out before the trial and use your memorandum to refresh your memory while interrogating the witness.

Avoid leading questions on direct examination. This is one of the greatest difficulties the young lawyer experiences in the interrogating of witnesses. He finds it hard to frame his questions in such manner as not to be subject to the objection that they are leading. The mastering of this phase of witness examination is more difficult than one would suppose. It usually comes only with experience. However, if you will acquire the habit of asking yourself each time you propound a question on direct examination "Is this question leading?" you will find that you gradually acquire the knack of keeping your questions from being subject to this vice. It is just a matter of constantly bearing in mind that leading questions are not permissible.

After the cross-examination of your witness by opposing counsel comes your redirect examination. Some lawyers, and especially those young in the practice, believe that it is always necessary to propound questions on re-direct examination. This is not true. If the cross-examination has not shaken the testimony of the witness and has not brought forward any new matter, and if your direct examination was full and complete and has elicited all of the testimony relevant to the issue, there is no point in asking any further questions. If the cross-examination has brought out any matter or thing that requires explanation or has injected into the case new matter not covered by your direct examination, then a re-direct examination is in order and sufficient questions should be asked to explain the matters requiring explanation or answer the additional points presented. The point here is that there is no reason for the asking of questions on re-direct examination merely because your adversary has completed his cross-examination and you are entitled to the last word. If there is nothing to be explained or added to the witness' testimony you should omit any additional questioning.

We now come to the cross-examination of your adversary's witnesses. Cross-examination is the most potent and deadly weapon that the trial lawyer has in his arsenal. The proper exercising of your right to lead your adversary's witnesses, to contradict them, to impeach them, to discredit them, oftentimes means the difference between victory and defeat. Many cases are won or lost on the cross-examination of witnesses. Helpful admissions elicited by you on cross-examination of your adversary's witnesses are sometimes far more important and beneficial than the testimony coming from your own witnesses. A jury is often more impressed with testimony favorable to you coming from the witnesses for the opposing side, and which you have brought out by your cross-examination, than they are by the testimony of your own witnesses. Too much thought, study and preparation cannot be given to the art of cross-examination. It is the most important single phase of the trial of a lawsuit.

In connection with your cross-examination of your opponent's witnesses, perhaps more than in any other part of the trial except the argument to the jury, should your demeanor be suited to your temperament. No false note must be struck here. If you are naturally dominant and aggressive, with a powerful and over-mastering personality, and an appearance and voice to match, then you may cross-examine witnesses in the "brow-beating" style – in the manner usually depicted in the motion pictures. If you are this type such method of cross-examination will be all right for you. It will be your natural manner, and such method, when natural and not assumed, and when supported by a powerful personality, is most effective. Such a cross-examiner can usually overwhelm and dominate most witnesses, and by sheer force of personality and sledge hammer tactics secure a desirable result. However, if you are not naturally of the dominant type, and few of us are, such method of procedure should be avoided, for it can only be successfully used by a person to whom it comes naturally and for whom a less aggressive attitude would be difficult to assume. For the more conservative type of temperament an entirely different method of approach is to be recommended. These lines are written primarily for the benefit of the young lawyer of average temperament, and not for the highly aggressive type, for the latter will not need such advice as is here given but will be a law unto himself in his career and will formulate his own rules of conduct and procedure as he goes along.

In the cross-examination of a witness your attitude ordinarily should be one of politeness. There is no reason for brusqueness unless the witness is patently misrepresenting the facts. In the beginning of your cross-examination you should conduct yourself in such manner as to give the witness the impression that you are being absolutely fair with him and that it is not your intention to embarrass him or question the truthfulness of what he has said. In other words, you should try and win his confidence; at least to the extent of having him believe that you are merely seeking to ascertain the facts and are not particularly interested in contradicting what he has said. Most witnesses expect to be treated harshly on cross-examination, and are inclined to be defiant and uncommunicative, but when they find your attitude to be one of friendliness and politeness they are usually disarmed and placed at ease, and your task in securing favorable answers from them is made much easier than it otherwise would be. Unless you are able to catch the witness in some palpable untruth, or are able to develop some point by his testimony that is highly detrimental to the opposition, it is well to continue this attitude of friendliness and politeness throughout your cross-examination. Of course, when such situations as are last mentioned develop you can then let yourself go and permit politeness to go by the board, for in such event there is little danger of injuring your cause by antagonizing the jury or losing the cooperation of the witness.

Ordinarily you can't go far wrong if you treat all witnesses with politeness and avoid abusive tactics. As is said by Dwight G. McCarty, when speaking of the examination of witnesses, "When you accuse them they resent it. When you flatter them they like it. When you antagonize them they fight you back. Molasses will catch more flies than vinegar. Good nature will catch more witnesses than anger or irritation."[13]

So much for your attitude and manner when cross-examining a witness. The next point for consideration is when you should cross-examine and when you should refrain therefrom, and the extent of your cross-examination. Some lawyers, and most beginners, think it imperative to cross-examine every witness placed on the stand by the opposition. This is not true. If the witness has not injured your side of the case by his testimony, there is no reason for questioning him at all on

---

[13] Dwight G. McCarty, "Psychology for the Lawyer." By permission of Prentice-Hall, Inc., publishers.

cross-examination. If you do so, you may bring out damaging testimony that would not otherwise have been developed. You may as well let well enough alone. If he hasn't hurt you let him go. On the other hand, if the witness' testimony has been damaging and you have reason to believe that you can weaken it by developing certain facts, then proceed with your cross-examination; being careful, however, to have a definite plan in mind and something definite to develop. There is nothing to be gained by asking the witness questions on cross-examination which do nothing more than rehash his testimony on direct examination; in fact such course of procedure is hurtful in that the witness' testimony is more firmly implanted in the minds of the jury. Never cross-examine merely because it is your turn.

Assuming that the witness' testimony is such as to require or justify cross-examination, then proceed therewith, but always with careful thought and purpose and with a definite goal in mind. You are on dangerous ground and aimless questioning may bring forth unanticipated answers of a highly detrimental nature. It has been said that a lawyer on cross-examination should never ask the witness a question unless he is certain of the answer or doesn't care what the answer may be. While rather extreme, this assertion is largely true. More or less random questions may be asked when you are beginning your cross-examination and attempting to lull the witness into a sense of security, but when you get to the material facts in the case be certain of your ground and confine your interrogation to questions that you are fairly certain will be answered in a manner favorable to you, or at least not detrimental to your cause.

The method to be used in eliciting testimony from a witness on cross-examination – the questions to be asked and the manner of asking – varies as much as does the types of witnesses encountered. Some general observations thought to be of a helpful nature may well be made at this point.

If the witness has told a straight-forward story on direct examination, there is no point to having him restate it on cross-examination. If you are going to cross-examine him you should question him with reference to collateral matters; matters which in themselves may not be of controlling importance in the lawsuit, but which may show bias or prejudice on his part, a faulty memory, or a variance between his testimony and that of other witnesses who have testified to the same general facts that he has covered by his testimony. You may be able to bring out testimony on cross-examination that shows that the witness is interested in the outcome of the case, or that he is in some manner close to one of the party litigants. Where the rule has been invoked and other witnesses have testified to the same state of facts out of the hearing of the witness on the stand, then he may well be interrogated as to all minute details surrounding the transaction. It is seldom that two witnesses can agree on all of the details of an occurrence. If you are able to bring out discrepancies in the testimony of the witnesses for the opposing side, even though they be with reference to matters not of controlling importance to the disposition of the case, you have succeeded to some extent in weakening their testimony. At least you have placed yourself in position to argue to the jury that if the witnesses were not in accord on these otherwise unimportant points, they are probably mistaken in their testimony on the real points at issue. Sometimes gratifying results are obtained by a line of questioning testing the memory of the witness, such as asking him the time and place of the occurrence of the event about which he has testified, the condition of the weather, a description of the surroundings, the persons present, their names, how they were dressed, and questions of a like nature. While such questions may be unimportant to the real issues in the case, they may elicit answers that tend to weaken the witness' testimony. If he does not remember the little things it may be well argued that he is mistaken in his version of the more important ones. The effect of the testimony of witnesses otherwise unimpeached has been at times totally destroyed by this method of interrogation on cross-examination.

With some witnesses, and particularly with fragile witnesses such as children, the unstable, those suffering from a disability, even highly emotional witnesses, and the like (the subject of cross-examination of such witnesses will be considered at some length further on), it is often possible to secure helpful testimony on cross-examination by making an appeal to the witness' sense of right and justice; by placing the witness on his honor, as it were. This can be done by reiterating from time to time during the cross-examination "I know you wish to be fair and that you do not wish to do anyone an injustice in this case, now isn't it true that" thus and so, and like remarks. Such complimentary approach is flattering to the witness and sometimes causes him to lean over backward in his effort to be fair. It sometimes produces surprisingly good results. Of course, whether you should use this method or not depends upon the type of witness that you are cross-examining. Some respond and some do not. If you start this method with a witness and it does not produce results drop it immediately, for the witness is one to whom such an approach does not appeal. As you gain experience in the trial of lawsuits you will grow to know intuitively when to pursue this course and when to refrain therefrom.

With other witnesses it is sometimes possible to conduct a successful cross-examination by being extremely friendly and good-natured; even somewhat jovial, if dignity is preserved and the proprieties are observed. With this type of witness a line of questioning – given in a smiling, friendly, intimate, wheedling manner – such as "Now you know that this is true don't you Mr. Brown" or

"There is no question about that is there Mr. Brown," and like interrogation, sometimes works wonders. Good natured people are usually susceptible to this method of approach. You can usually determine from the witness' appearance and from his answers to the questions propounded to him on direct examination whether or not he is a person of such pleasant disposition that you would be justified in approaching him in the manner here suggested.

Then, of course, there is the determined witness who has told his story and is going to stick to it, and who considers your every question a reflection upon his integrity. It is useless to attempt to appeal to his sense of fairness or his good nature. With him you may as well follow the orthodox method of cross-examination. Sometimes it is possible to weaken the testimony of such a witness in the eyes of the jury by playing upon and bringing out the decided nature of his character to such extent that the jury may be caused to mistake such resoluteness for a personal interest in the case being tried.

Where you have matter or information which places you in a position to impeach the testimony of an adverse witness, then you are indeed in a happy position, and may cross-examine with a feeling of certainty and a measure of security. It is in this type of situation that cross-examination plays such an important, if not controlling part in the trial of a case. You have in your possession, we will say, a letter written by the witness or a statement signed by him. How best to approach the subject? Some lawyers always handle the matter in the same way. They will produce the document and say to the witness "Did you not make this statement," reading a part or all of the document to the witness. The witness immediately realizes that he is being impeached by his prior statement, and becomes evasive and attempts to find a way out. He begins to explain and sometimes to deny the writing and often the effect of the impeaching matter is lessened and sometimes destroyed. In certain cases this approach may be a proper one. However, by and large, it is thought that a more subtle method should be used. In most cases it is better to produce the writing and say to the witness in a friendly, conversational tone, "Now I have here a writing signed by you. I am not trying particularly to contradict what you have testified

57

to. I just want to see if I can refresh your memory about the matter. In this writing you said thus and so, did you not?" Usually when approached in such a manner, the witness does not realize that he is being impeached, and will readily admit the contents of the writing and will admit the correctness thereof. All you are trying to do is to show that the witness made a statement in writing contrary to his testimony on the stand. By this gentle approach you have lulled the witness into a sense of security and have got him to admit the writing. You can impress upon the jury the enormity of the witness' lapse from truthfulness in your argument.

There is yet another thing to be mentioned with reference to the impeaching of a witness' testimony, and that is that you should not go too far. Prove your point by your cross-examination of the witness and then reserve for your argument your criticism of his untruthfulness. Even though you have established by your interrogation of the witness that he has not told the truth do not take him to task too strongly before the jury. Human nature is a peculiar thing, and if you are too vehement in your handling of the witness the jury may be caused to sympathize with him, even though they know that he has falsified.

There is always a great temptation to excoriate a witness when you have proven absolutely that he is not telling the truth, and sometimes such a course is in order. However, usually moderation is the best policy; at least it is always less dangerous.

We now get to the matter of the cross-examination of fragile witnesses, leaving them somewhat more vulnerable fragile on the witness stand. Lawyers have been writing on this subject for many years. All of them urge great caution in cross-examining such witness; some even go so far as to say that such witnesses should never be cross-examined under any circumstances.

In truth, fragile witnesses do make difficult witnesses, and on cross-examination must be treated with great politeness and handled with caution. Yet there is no reason why a lawyer should not cross-examine them. More courtesy and consideration must be shown to them and more tact exercised than is ordinarily the case, but aside from this they should be cross-examined when the occasion requires just as are other witnesses.

Just as in dealing with any child, great care should be exercised to the end that the jury may not get the impression that the fragile witness is being abused or that the examiner is taking an unfair advantage. When this is done, and when the fragile witness is treated with politeness and courtesy, you should feel just as free to cross-examine as in the case of any other witness. In fact if a fragile witness is approached on cross-examination in the ingenuous manner suggested earlier in this chapter, better results are sometimes obtained than from other witnesses.

One other word of caution in the matter of cross-examination. No matter how well things are going do not attempt to parade before the jury your ability or knowledge or your keenness as a cross-examiner. In other words do not attempt to "show off." Even though you are succeeding in destroying the witness, you may not be making the impression on the jury that you desire. An actual occurrence may be mentioned as an illustration of what is here meant. A young lawyer who was quite learned in medicine was cross-examining an elderly doctor. It soon became apparent that he knew more about the subject being discussed than did the witness. He was rapidly taking the old doctor apart. However, in the midst of the cross-examination one of the jurors rose in the jury box and requested the Court to be permitted to ask a question. Being told that, he might he said "I want to know if this lawyer is really seeking information by his questions or if he is just trying to show how smart he is."

In dealing with witnesses try to be reasonably fair, always be courteous and polite, think before you speak, have a purpose when propounding your questions, do not ask questions merely to be talking, and you will be all right.

6. THE TRIAL

In this chapter we will consider the trial of your case in its entirety. The matters of jury selection, the handling of your witnesses and the making of your argument to the jury are covered in detail in other chapters but will in some respects be alluded to here.

After you and your opponent have announced yourselves ready for trial the first step in the proceedings is to select a jury. A panel of prospective jurors is placed before you. Their number varies in different jurisdictions, but there are always more of them than the twelve that will finally be selected. This in order that you and your adversary may exercise your challenges and eliminate from the list the jurors you do not want. You have the right to challenge for cause, and thus eliminate from the panel any juror who is disqualified under the law to sit on the jury in your case. In addition to this right you are granted a certain number of peremptory challenges; that is to say challenges by virtue of which you may eliminate from the panel, at your discretion and without having to assign any reason therefor, a given number of jurors. The number of peremptory challenges to which you are entitled varies in different jurisdictions, but in civil cases it is usually three or six.

In most jurisdictions you are permitted to make a preliminary statement to the jury panel in order to inform the prospective jurors of the nature of the case and the contentions of the parties, and are further permitted to interrogate each juror separately. In some jurisdictions, and in most of the Federal Courts, all communications with the jury panel are had through the trial Judge, and you are not permitted to speak to or question the jurors directly. Where you are permitted to address the jurors directly you should at the very outset, by your statement and, if necessary, by the form of your questions, get before them as forcefully as possible and to as great an extent as the proprieties will permit what your contentions are in the case. As is said by Mr. Francis L. Wellman, "First, through careful selection of questions the voir dire should place before the entire court room your whole story and the fundamental basis upon which your position rests."[14] In other words, begin the trial of your case and start your efforts to make a favorable impression of yourself and your cause on the jury with the very first word you utter in the courtroom.

After the jury panel has been interrogated, all challenges exercised, the jury selected and placed in the jury box, and the jurors have been duly sworn to try the cause, the next step is the reading or stating of the pleadings, and in some jurisdictions the making of a statement of the case. The reading of the pleadings or statement of the case should not be done in a perfunctory manner. You should here again exercise your abilities to "sell" yourself and your cause to the jury. You should speak in a clear voice, loud enough to be heard without difficulty by all of the jury, and should enunciate your words carefully and with force and emphasis. In the matter of reading your pleadings, when you reach such parts that you consider to be of particular importance it is well to pause from time to time and look at the jury in

---

[14] Francis L. Wellman, "Success in Court." By permission of The MacMillan Company, Publishers.

order that they may be given the impression that something significant has been stated. Do not read your pleadings in a hasty manner and a monotonous tone of voice. Try and put life into your effort. When making a preliminary statement to the jury, do so as if you were arguing the case on its merits. In other words, even in this preliminary step in the trial try to "put over" your own personality and your case to the jury.

After the reading or stating of the pleadings, and the statement to the jury where such is permitted, the next step in the proceedings is the introduction of the testimony of the witnesses. In another chapter we have considered in detail the handling of the witnesses, both your own and those of your adversary. There will here be made various observations with reference to your conduct during that part of the trial when the testimony is being introduced and up until the closing of the evidence.

As has been previously said, your attitude throughout the trial should be one of dignity and seriousness. You should be polite and courteous to your adversary, to the trial Judge and the witnesses. You should seek to create the impression with the jury that your only thought and desire is to have the absolute truth brought out and determined. You should seek to impress them with your sincerity and should at all times exhibit an apparent feeling of absolute confidence. If you do not exhibit a feeling of confidence in yourself and in your cause you cannot expect the jury to have confidence in you. No matter how badly things are going for you do not show by your words or manner that you are perturbed. The jury is not trained in the law and sometimes will not grasp the significance of an occurrence, even though it may be extremely harmful to you, unless you show by your conduct that you have been hurt. Maintain a "poker face" throughout.

The matter of making objections to the introduction of testimony is one for serious consideration. Frivolous objections upon your part, or the making of a great many objections, may hurt your cause with the jury. If too many objections to testimony are made the jury may assume that you are attempting to conceal the facts. If groundless objections are made and are overruled by the Court the jury may get the impression that you do not know what you are doing. Most beginners are prone to make too many objections to testimony.

They will object on the slightest ground and thus tend to irritate the Judge and jury. Furthermore it is not always proper to object even though a question or answer may be legally inadmissible. It may be something that, even though inadmissible, does not hurt your cause. Do not object to testimony that is harmless to you merely to show your knowledge of the law. There is nothing to be gained by following this procedure. The truth is that the fewer objections you have to urge upon the trial the better impression you make upon the jury.

If you will follow these suggestions with reference to objections to testimony you can't go far wrong and you will run little risk of irritating the jury or lessening your standing in their eyes: Seldom make an objection unless you know that you are right and are reasonably certain that the trial Judge will sustain it, or if he overrules it, that you have really accomplished something by preserving a point of error. The constant urging of objections which are not well taken and having them overruled by the trial Judge may cause the jury to believe that you do not know the law or that the Court is against you. Furthermore, if you make objection to a question and it is overruled and then a damaging   answer is given by the witness it will likely make a stronger impression on the jury than it otherwise would, for by your objection you have "highlighted" the matter and concentrated the jury's attention on the situation and they will attach more importance to it than they would had the question been asked and the answer given without objection. If you follow the practice of objecting only when you know that you are right, your objections will usually be sustained and the jury will be impressed with the fact that you know what you are doing, or may be led to believe that the trial Judge looks with favor upon your side of the case. Then, too, if such well taken objections are overruled you have your points of error. While, of course, you must endeavor to keep out of the record hurtful testimony that is inadmissible, you should make only such objections during the trial as are necessary to achieve this end. If the testimony is not hurting your side of the case there is no point in objecting even though your objections may be good. While your adversary has no right to lead his witnesses, still there is not much necessity for objecting to his questions if the answers of the witness are not harmful to you. Try and avoid creating the impression that you are objecting to any and everything that occurs, for the jury knows nothing of the niceties of the law and may get the idea that you are attempting to "obstruct justice." If the trial Judge rules against you on an objection do not argue the point with him unless you are in position to produce authority and convince him then and there that he is wrong. Such argument, unless immediately supported by authority, is usually fruitless, and not only does it not help you with the Judge but may injure you in the eyes of the jury in leading them to believe more strongly than ever that you are not proficient. When forced to object do so in a quiet, dignified manner. Do not show great concern or excitement or the jury may get the impression that the testimony you are attempting to exclude is something of great importance. If you will follow the same quiet procedure in making all objections, the jury will not be able to detect from your attitude what is important and what is not. State your objections clearly and concisely and be certain that they are correctly reflected in the record.

When you are trying a case in a jurisdiction where exceptions are necessary to preserve points of error, if your objection to testimony is overruled, state that you except to the ruling of the Court and ordinarily let the matter stop there. In such jurisdictions as are last mentioned, be certain that your exception is noted in the record.

An illustration of the harmful effect of making too many objections during the trial comes to mind. The lawyer for the defendant in an action for damages for death made many objections throughout the trial. As the jury was filing out of the jury box on their way to the jury room he heard one of the jurors remarking to another in a sarcastic tone of voice, "I object, I object." The jury brought in a verdict against him for $40,000.00. While, of course, the lawyer's objections did not of themselves produce this result, the attitude of the juror mentioned indicates clearly that such course of action did not help his side of the case with the jury.

In the interrogation of witnesses do not ask questions that you know are legally improper or that call for answers which you know are inadmissible in evidence. It is considered quite smart upon the part of some lawyers to ask questions, the answers to which they know are inadmissible in evidence, either for the purpose of getting such improper matter before the jury by the asking of the question, or for the purpose of placing opposing counsel in a bad light before the jury by forcing him to object. This practice cannot be too strongly condemned, for while it may not be unethical it is certainly unfair and if pursued over a period of time will give you the reputation of being a "sharp" practitioner. Furthermore such course of procedure is dangerous, for cases are sometimes reversed by the Appellate Courts merely because an improper question is asked and even though objection is sustained and the jury instructed not to consider the matter.

In the progress of the trial be as agreeable as possible with your adversary without being familiar. If he is attempting to prove some fact which is not of controlling importance and which you know to be true it is sometimes well to state to the Court that you agree that such fact is true, thus saving the time and trouble of making such proof. Such action on your part places you in a favorable light with the Court and jury and if such practice is followed over a period of time helps you build up friendly relations with your fellow attorneys. There is no point to compelling your adversary to go to the trouble of proving something that is undisputed.

In the trial of your case refrain from "flirting" with the jury and attempting to ingratiate yourself with them by a servile attitude or a flattering approach. By your attitude throughout the trial seek to impress upon them that they, as well as you, are engaged in a serious and dignified undertaking and that the entire proceeding is an effort to arrive at a just decision of the controversy. Do not be too complimentary. Do not evidence too much concern for their comfort. Take the position that you are presenting your case to them as officers of the court, sworn to do their duty without fear or favor, and that you are asking a favorable verdict not because of your charm but because your cause is meritorious.

In the trial of your case avoid all side bar remarks. Always address yourself either to the Judge, the witness or the jury. There is seldom any need for your addressing any remarks to opposing counsel during the trial, and as has been elsewhere observed such a practice sometimes leads to unpleasant results. If the conduct of opposing counsel is objectionable make your objections to the Court. Avoid bickering. If your adversary addresses you in unpleasant terms do not respond in kind. Maintain your temper and your dignity. Do not attempt to exhibit your skill at repartee. While practice of this kind may elicit mirth or other evidence of apparent appreciation from the jury, it really does no good in the long run but only tends to obscure the issues in the case. As is said by the late Emory R. Buckner, who was an outstanding trial lawyer in New York City, "All colloquy with opposing counsel, all repartee or 'wise cracking,' every tendency to show that you are as smart and as bright and as witty as the other fellow should be strictly avoided. The successful trial lawyer will sit and suffer under abuse and smart remarks and keep his tongue tight no matter how good an answer he may think of, and always be thinking of his client. This is one of the hardest things for a trial lawyer to learn."[15] After all, the winning of your case is

---

[15] Francis L. Wellman, "Success in Court." By permission of The MacMillan Company, Publishers.

the matter of first concern and not the exhibition of your smartness. Do not be afraid of the jury. You are in effect placed on exhibition before the twelve people in the box and at first you are inclined to feel ill at ease and embarrassed. Always remember that the jurors are themselves in an atmosphere extremely alien to them and are even more ill at ease than you are. If you will keep this fact constantly in mind during the trial of a case you will find that you are more sure of yourself than you otherwise would be.

In conducting your case be particularly careful not to do or say anything that may bring about a reprimand from the Court. Such reprimands by the trial Judge are most embarrassing and do not help you in the eyes of the jury. If you will be careful to observe the suggestions made hereinbefore with reference to rising when addressing the trial Judge, avoiding argument with him over his rulings, refraining from side bar remarks and unnecessary conversation with your adversary, and like matters, you should have no difficulty on this score.

It is generally considered that the best way for the young lawyer to "learn the ropes" in court is to sit with a seasoned trial lawyer through the trial of many cases and observe the method of procedure employed by him in order that his tactics may be emulated. This procedure is all right so far as it goes, but the truth of the matter is that the beginner learns more by trying one case alone and on his own responsibility than he does by "sitting in" on the trial of a number of cases tried by others. Ordinarily the proficient and experienced trial lawyer tries his case with such outward appearing ease and lack of effort that the beginner does not realize the innumerable legal obstacles and pitfalls that are present but that are being skillfully avoided. Few questions of the admissibility of evidence or other matters of trial procedure arise in such case because the experienced lawyer is proceeding in such manner that they are avoided. Consequently the young lawyer may arrive at the conclusion that it is all as easy as it looks, and finds to his surprise that many difficulties that he had not thought of present themselves when he is on his own. It is thought by some lawyers highly skilled in trial work that the better practice is for the beginner to take over the responsibility of the trial of his lawsuits from the very outset and learn by the method of trial and error; that by following this course he learns more in less time. Certainly when the young lawyer is confronted with a trial problem which he has to work out for himself and without assistance, he will always remember that particular point of law, and thus over a period of time he will become proficient in his own right and without a great deal of help from others. In this regard the statement of an actual occurrence may not be out of order. A young lawyer who had sat through the trial of a number of cases with an experienced trial lawyer undertook to try his first case by himself, the case being one identical in character and presenting the same questions that were involved in the others in which he had participated. He encountered many difficulties, and upon the conclusion of his case was constrained to remark to the older lawyer, "When you tried those cases everything went off so smoothly that I didn't realize that there were any problems involved. However, when I tried my case I found that I was at a loss most of the time. I had seen you take care of identical situations, but did not know why you were pursuing the course you did, and when I was confronted with the same situation I didn't know what to do." As stated before it is all right to begin your court experience by sitting through trials with experienced lawyers, but you will learn more in less time by starting to try cases by yourself as soon as you can.

If you are collaborating with another lawyer in the trial of a lawsuit never make suggestions to him while he is interrogating a witness and never permit him to make suggestions to you at such time. If you are trying the case alone do not permit your client to make suggestions to you during the time that you are examining a witness. There is nothing more disconcerting in the trial of a lawsuit than to be developing the testimony of a witness in accordance with your own line of thought, and then have someone break in with a suggested question foreign to the matter that you are attempting to develop. In interrogating a witness a lawyer may have in mind a purpose not immediately apparent from his questions. He should not have his train of thought broken by suggestions from others who may be following an entirely different line of thought. This is a matter more important than may appear at first consideration, for it sometimes happens that the interrogator, preoccupied with his efforts to develop a certain line of testimony by his interrogation, may throw in a question at the suggestion of one sitting with him in the trial, the answer to which may destroy what he is attempting to build up, or be hurtful in some other regard. The best practice to follow is for the client or the collaborating attorney to write down such ideas or suggested questions that occur to him during the time that the interrogation of the witness is in progress, and then, after the lawyer who is questioning the witness is through, make his suggestions as to additional questions that he thinks should be asked.

In the trial of a lawsuit there is a constant spiritual struggle for dominance on the part of the lawyers on either side of the case. It isn't evident to the eye but it can always be felt. You should endeavor to be the dominating personality if possible. To do this, always attempt to create the impression that you are at all times master of the situation. Try not to show any faltering or indecision. Appear confident, certain and cheerful throughout the trial and let nothing that occurs shake your poise.

7. THE ARGUMENT

The evidence has been completed and both sides have rested. The next step in the trial of your case is the preparation of the Court's charge or instructions to the jury. The matter of the preparation of the charge of the Court will not be discussed here because it is purely a matter of legal procedure. In some jurisdictions the Court's charge to the jury is given orally, in others it is given in writing; in some jurisdictions it is given before the argument of the attorneys to the jury, in others it is given subsequent to such argument. What we are concerned with here is not the legal technicalities of the Court's charge but the argument you are to make to the jury in an effort to convince them of the justness of your case and prevail upon them to return a verdict in your favor.

Enough has previously been said about your general attitude of seriousness, dignity and courteous behavior. It is obvious that this attitude must be continued and preserved during your argument to the jury. When you stand up before the jury to make your argument try and assume as easy and natural a posture as possible. It is well to stand in one place throughout the argument, for constant moving about tends to distract the attention of the jury. If you do move about do so slowly and deliberately. Avoid jerky movements. You will probably find at first that the disposition of your hands presents somewhat of a problem. It is usually said that one should forget his hands when talking to an audience. However, this is easier said than done. If you experience much trouble in this connection it is well to occupy your hands by holding a paper or some other object in them, or to keep them clasped, either before or behind you, or–although this practice is usually frowned upon–you may keep your hands in the side pockets of your coat. Be certain to speak in a distinct tone of voice, loud enough to be heard at all times by all of the members of the jury. Do not speak too rapidly. When you reach the important parts of your talk it is well to speak slowly and deliberately. Ordinarily the members of the jury are not extremely alert mentally, and if you speak too rapidly they may fail to follow and understand the thought that you are expressing. Whether you should make your argument throughout in a conversational tone of voice or should do so in an oratorical manner depends upon your own temperament, the type of case you are trying and particular situations that may arise. This feature of your argument will be spoken of at some length later on.

Do not be unduly perturbed if you are nervous when making your argument to the jury. You may be the type that will never get over this feeling of nervousness when delivering a public address. This does not mean that you will not be able to make a good speech. A careful observer can often observe a trembling of the hands or detect a tremor in the voice of experienced lawyers when beginning their address to a jury; sometimes lawyers who have been trying lawsuits and making arguments for a lifetime. The late William Jennings Bryan, who probably delivered as many public addresses in his lifetime as any person in history once remarked during his late years that he had never risen before an audience to deliver a speech but that he experienced a weakness in his knees and a sick feeling in his stomach. The feeling of nervousness incident to public speaking ordinarily disappears after a few minutes. With some persons it persists throughout the address. If you are this type of person do not be unduly concerned, for it is merely indicated that you are of a high-strung temperament. The chances are that you will do better at public speaking than if you were of a more phlegmatic type. If you are bothered too much by the trembling of your hands it is well to hold something in them, or keep them clasped, or place them in your pockets, as before observed, for you should, of course, attempt to conceal your nervousness as far as possible. If the jury detects that you are nervous you are not helped in building up with them that feeling of confidence in you that has been spoken of previously.

Now you are confronted with the question that gives all young lawyers concern: What manner of argument should you make to a jury? Should you deliver your address in a calm, collected, earnest manner and in a conversational tone of voice, or should you resort to invective and declaim passionately before the jury? While most writers on the subject are in accord in saying that the first method is the desirable one and, in this day and time, probably the only one that should be used, it cannot be gainsaid that with the proper lawyer and the proper case or occasion, the latter method is sometimes both appropriate and effective. The statement has been made that a lawyer arguing a case to a jury occupies more or less the same position as a salesman attempting to sell a bill of goods; that in such a case the salesman would not attempt to make a sale by storming and raging at his prospect and that hence the lawyer is no more justified in following such a course. It has been further said that logic is more persuasive than noise, which is indubitably true. It must be admitted that storming and raging before a jury is seldom desirable. However forcefulness of expression is not to be entirely overlooked. The aggressive approach has its place in the proper case and if used by the proper person.

The question largely resolves itself down to the matter of individual temperament, which subject has been previously discussed. If you are the dominant, aggressive type with a strong personality and it is natural for you to express yourself forcefully, then deliver your argument in a forceful or even impassioned manner if you desire. It will be natural to you and you will not be giving the impression of theatricalism. In fact it will be difficult for you to do otherwise. If, on the other hand, you are of the average temperament then you had best confine yourself to the more conservative type of argument, only resorting to extreme forcefulness of utterance when you are actually and sincerely moved thereto by matters or situations that present themselves. Even though you are of the quiet and conservative type you will sometimes be confronted with situations that so arouse your honest indignation that you feel the necessity of expressing yourself in vehement terms. When such an occasion arises, and your feeling is genuine, yield to it and express yourself with such vehemence and emotion as your feelings in the matter dictate. In such a case you will be acting naturally and your sincerity will be manifest to the jury. The point to remember is never to assume a forcefulness and emotionalism of delivery that you do not actually feel.

While on this point it may be observed that some successful trial lawyers always deliver their arguments to juries in the "shouting" manner, while on the other hand other trial lawyers who are equally successful never raise their voices above the conversational tone when addressing the jury.

Thus it will be seen that there is no set rule; that it cannot be said with certainty that the conservative method of approach is the only one to be followed under all circumstances. It is thought, as is indicated hereinbefore, that the matter is largely one of individual temperament; that what is becoming and convincing in one person would be inappropriate and unconvincing in another. At all events you should not endeavor to pattern your conduct after that of other lawyers you encounter merely because they are successful before juries, for their method may be entirely inappropriate in your case. What you should do is to determine for yourself which type of approach comes natural to you and is most suited to your temperament. In other words, as is said elsewhere, be yourself at all times, and particularly when addressing the jury.

When delivering your address it is well to turn your gaze from time to time from one juror to another. Unless there is a very good reason for it you should not address yourself to one juror, as is sometimes done unconsciously. During the argument, try to look at each juror at least once. You do not want to leave the impression that you are slighting any of them. Try and avoid as much as possible the reading of matter to the jury. This prevents you from looking at them as you are talking. There are occasions, of course, when documents or excerpts therefrom must be read to the jury in argument, but this should be reduced to a minimum, for juries are inclined to pay little attention to matters of this kind and usually lose interest very quickly.

Do not "talk down" to a jury. While most of the jurors will probably not be on the same intellectual level as you are, there is no reason for your assuming a style of delivery or a choice of words that is not natural to you. Some lawyers are of the opinion that in arguing to a jury the use of bad grammar, slang and colloquialisms is necessary in order that the jury may be given the impression that the lawyer is "just one of them," and that purity of speech and pronunciation should be avoided. This is not true. If you are careful in your choice of words and use good grammar in ordinary conversation do not fear being equally as careful in your argument to a jury. There is no reason for your attempting to change your natural manner of speech, and it is useless for you to try for you will not be able to mislead the jury. If you wish to use poetic quotations or classical illustrations, do so. Do not fear that they will be "over the heads" of the jurors. The truth is that even though some of the jurors may not understand everything you say, they are likely to appreciate your efforts, for you are in effect complimenting their mental capacities. While, of course, you must avoid giving any impression of being one of the elect or a pedant, still it is not necessary for you to try to appear to be just "one of the boys," for, as has been before observed, and as you should always remember, the jurors do not expect you to be as they are in all particulars but expect you to be a person of learning and on a higher intellectual plane than the average person. You can hardly prejudice yourself in their eyes by exhibiting qualities that they expect you to possess.

As is indicated in another chapter, unless you are naturally of a humorous turn of mind and inclined to be witty it is best to avoid all funny stories and humorous remarks when making your argument to the jury. There are some lawyers who can tell humorous stories and make witty remarks to a jury during argument and do it gracefully and with pleasing effect. However, such people are few in number, and unless you are naturally inclined in that direction it is best to leave the wit and humor to them. Ordinarily an attempt at humor in argument to a jury, unless by an expert, gets little visible response from the jurors. This perhaps for the reason that the jurors, even though amused, feel that they should not evidence such fact. When humor is attempted by the lawyer addressing a jury and the jurors give no outward evidence of their appreciation, the lawyer is made to feel somewhat foolish, which feeling may have a deleterious effect on the remainder of his argument.

In the making of your argument it is well, just as in a political campaign, to mention the lawyer opposing you as seldom as possible. There is usually little reason for mentioning or discussing your opponent. Avoid criticizing him or his tactics as much as possible, for if you go too far you may cause the jury to sympathize with him. This does not mean, of course, that you should avoid criticism or condemnation of the opposing lawyer where it is clearly developed that he has attempted to mislead the jury or has been in some manner patently unfair. However, this seldom occurs in a lawsuit, and ordinarily such criticism should be avoided. If you mention your opponent too often in your argument the jury may get the impression that he is quite an important person and may pay him more attention than they otherwise would.

Do not be too much concerned during your argument over the apparent lack of interest being shown by some of the jurors. Sometimes during jury argument a juror will sit with his eyes closed, as if asleep, or will appear to be preoccupied with his own thoughts, or by some other conduct exhibit an apparent indifference to what you are saying. While sometimes this attitude on the part of a juror does denote real indifference, usually it is but the juror's own peculiar way of concentrating upon what is being said, and often such a juror is following you more carefully than others who are apparently paying close attention to your argument.

Never under any circumstances knowingly misquote the record when making a jury argument and never attempt to mislead the jury. You will seldom succeed in such an effort, and if the jury once gets the impression that you are not being frank and honest with them your chances of winning a verdict at their hands are greatly reduced. In the matter of misquoting the record, always remember that twelve jurors have heard the testimony and that while you may be able to deceive some of them, the chances are that others among the twelve jurors will remember the particular point and know that you are misstating the facts. While you may be able to mislead some of the jurors in the box, the law of averages is such that it is most unlikely that you will succeed in misleading all of them, and any one of them who recognizes the fact that you are in error and are not being candid is likely to be against you in the deliberations in the jury room.

There is one particular thing that you should always bear in mind. Never underrate the intelligence of the jury. The late newspaper columnist, Raymond Clapper, once said in speaking of the American people that you should never overrate their knowledge or underrate their intelligence. This observation applies with particular force to a jury. The majority of the jurors sitting in the trial of a case are not usually people of learning; ordinarily the education of most of them is quite limited. However, this does not mean that they are not intelligent. They have just not had the opportunity of acquiring knowledge. The chances are that their perceptions and understanding of the ordinary things of life are as keen and their judgment as good, if not better, than that of highly educated persons. They can usually be depended upon to have "horse sense," and they are not easily deceived. When making your argument always allow for the lack of higher education on the part of most of the jurors, but do not patronize them or assume that they do not have a high order of intelligence.

At the outset of your career as a trial lawyer it is imperative that you make a study of the decisions dealing with improper jury argument. You will find that the field of proper jury argument is more limited than you would first assume. There are many things said in argument to a jury that the Courts hold to be improper and to constitute reversible error that would not occur to you off hand as being erroneous or improper. The restrictions imposed by the Courts on jury argument vary in severity in different jurisdictions. In some the rules are quite strict and many cases are reversed because of jury argument held to be improper. In others the regulations are more lenient and great latitude is permitted. You should not undertake jury argument until you are familiar with the decisions in your own jurisdiction dealing with the subject. It is quite disheartening to have your case reversed on appeal because of some inadvertent remark or statement that you made to the jury during your argument, particularly when your record is otherwise entirely clear of error. Such an occurrence is humiliating because it is something over which you had absolute control and which you did yourself; you can't comfort yourself by placing the responsibility on the Judge, the jury, or the witnesses, as you ordinarily may do where other types of error are involved.

Finally, when you have said everything to the jury in argument that you have to say, stop. Do not continue talking when you have exhausted your subject merely because you have not consumed the entire time allotted to you. Many young lawyers think that the longer speech they make to the jury the greater ability is shown, and that it denotes a lack of skill as a trial lawyer to make a short argument or complete the argument before the full time allowed is consumed. This is not the case. An argument directed sharply to the points at issue, even though short, is more effective than a long rambling talk. As is advised above, when you have said what you have to say, sit down.

8. THE APPELLATE COURT

You have won or lost your case in the lower court and now find yourself in the Appellate Court, either as the lawyer for the appealing litigant or the respondent. A few words of advice may well be given with reference to your course of conduct in this court.

It is to be assumed that you have carefully and painstakingly covered every point in your case in the written brief which you have prepared and filed in the Appellate Court. You are now before the Court for the purpose of presenting oral argument. You may ask "Why present oral argument when I have already covered every point in the case by my written brief?" The answer may well be stated as being that a lawyer is usually able to express himself more forcefully in oral argument than he can in his brief; he can "highlight" or emphasize points to better advantage; he can exhibit such enthusiasm or confidence in his contentions as cannot be done on the written page; by colloquy with the Judges he is able to explain quickly and clearly questions that may occur to them and which he could not anticipate when preparing his brief, and, finally, it may be said that there is no mode or means of communication yet devised by man that is as effective as a face to face talk.

Most Appellate Court Judges agree that oral argument is of great assistance to them and will advise you that you should seldom waive your right to make such argument. At least one Appellate Court Judge has stated that he and his colleagues usually hold an informal discussion immediately after hearing the oral argument in a case and arrive at a tentative decision based upon such argument, and further said that it was very seldom that such tentative opinion was changed by the Judges after reading the record and the briefs in the case. Another great Appellate Court Judge, when speaking of the desirability of oral argument, once said that, in his case at least, the fire and enthusiasm of the advocate in oral argument tended to excite his interest in the questions of law presented in a manner that could not be approached by any mere written brief. Most Appellate Court Judges welcome oral argument; they consider it helpful and do not feel that it is something to be endured. Hence you should make a practice of arguing orally all cases that you have in the Appellate Courts.

The Appellate Court Judges vary in number in different jurisdictions. Usually the number is three, seven or nine. The atmosphere of the Appellate Court is usually much more dignified and impressive than is that of the trial court. In the making of your argument you stand before the Judges at a lectern or table placed immediately in front of the judicial bench and facing the Chief Justice, who occupies a chair behind and in the center of the bench, the other Judges being seated on either side of him. In some state courts, and in all Federal Appellate Courts, the Justices wear robes. This, of course, adds additional solemnity to the setting and occasion. All in all you will find the environment very impressive, and at first you may feel ill at ease. However, after you have argued a few cases in the Appellate Courts and have discovered that the Judges possess no supernatural abilities you will lose this feeling.

Enough has previously been said in this book with reference to your attitude and demeanor while in court. Suffice to say here that while arguing your case in the Appellate Court you should be even more quiet, dignified and respectful, if such is possible, than you are in the trial court.

In presenting your argument to the Court you should express yourself clearly and choose your language with care. While you should be forceful in your presentation, the Appellate Court is no place for flights of oratory, or vehement and impassioned utterances. If you are one of the aggressive, dominant types previously spoken of, this is one time and place that you should endeavor to control your natural impulses. The presentation of your argument in a calm manner and a conversational tone of voice is the end to be sought.

You should, in the short time allotted to you for your argument, endeavor by all means within your power to make a favorable and lasting impression on the Judges of the court. Usually the oral argument is made before the Judges have read the record and the briefs and is the first they hear of the case. First impressions are long-lasting and are difficult to eradicate from the mind. The impression which the Judges get from your argument is their first impression in the proceedings and is one that will likely remain with them throughout their later consideration and study of the case. It is of paramount importance that you make this first impression a favorable one. To this end spare no effort in preparing yourself for the argument. Even though it will necessarily be short it is as important, in its way, as any other phase of the appeal.

In the presenting of your argument do not, except in rare instances, read from your brief. In most Appellate Courts the rules provide that briefs shall not be read by the lawyers during oral argument. Sometimes you may consider it necessary to read some short excerpt from your brief. If this occurs ask the Court's permission in advance to do so and reduce such reading to a minimum. There should be little reason for your reading from your brief anyway, for it is on file with the Court and will be read by the Judges. Try and avoid reading anything to the Court if you can do so. Do not read from the record unless it is absolutely necessary. Familiarize yourself with the record to such extent that you are able to state from memory such parts of it as you wish to call to the attention of the Court. If you are compelled to read from the record do so sparingly.

The time permitted you for argument in the Appellate Court is usually very limited when compared with the time granted for argument to the jury in the trial court. Usually the lawyer who is appealing the case is allowed thirty minutes to open the argument, his adversary is allowed thirty minutes to answer and then the appealing lawyer is allowed fifteen minutes to close the argument. While the time allotted differs with different courts this is about the average. It is obvious that you have very little time to present your case. Consequently you must be prepared to make each word count. Ordinarily you will have many points or counterpoints of error in your brief and it will be impossible to present all of them in the time allotted for oral argument. Select the points that you think most important and present them to the Court. It is better to present a few strong points fully and carefully than it is to present a great many in a cursory manner.

If you are representing the appealing party litigant, you should begin your argument by making a brief statement of the nature of the case and the points of law involved. You should state to the Court "This is a suit for the recovery of property in which the plaintiff prevailed and the defendant has appealed," or "This is an action for damages for death in which the defendant prevailed and the plaintiff has appealed," or a like terse statement descriptive of your case, thus informing the Court at the outset and in as brief a manner as possible just what the lawsuit is about and which litigant prevailed in the trial court and which is appealing the cause. Some lawyers seem to be of the opinion that in stating to the Appellate Court the nature and result of the suit in the trial court a resume of the case must be given. This is wholly unnecessary, and in fact time will not permit such course of procedure. Unless the appeal involves a question of the sufficiency of the evidence to raise or support a finding of fact by the trial court or jury it is seldom necessary to mention the evidence. That is to say, you need not inform the Court of the nature of the testimony on behalf of the plaintiff or what the defendant's witnesses testified to, or matters of like nature. Where there is involved a point of law which requires for its determination a consideration by the Appellate

Court of the evidence in the case, the discussion of such evidence may be pretermitted until you reach in your argument the presentation of the particular point of law to which such evidence is pertinent. At all events a discussion of the evidence is out of place in your preliminary statement to the Court.

After having informed the Court of the nature of the case, you should then tell the Court what points of law are involved; just what errors you are contending were committed by the trial court. As in the case of your statement of the nature and result of the suit, your statement of the points of law, or errors of which you complain, should be very brief.

If you have followed the course outlined, the Court is now informed of the nature of the case and the result of the trial and the points of law upon which you are relying for a reversal. You may then proceed with a discussion of each of your points of law in the order in which you stated them to the Court and attempt to persuade the Court that you are correct in your contentions in connection with each point.

If you are representing the respondent you will usually confine your argument to answering the contentions made by your opponent in his opening argument. The Court has already been made acquainted with the nature of the case and the points of law involved, and there is no necessity for your mentioning these matters unless some misstatement has been made. In such event you will tell the Court the correct situation. You will then proceed to answer the argument made by your adversary on the various law points presented by him. He has attempted to convince the Court by his argument that error was committed by the trial court in the particulars urged by him; you will endeavor to convince the Court that, under the law, there was no error in the particulars mentioned. With the difference in this paragraph noted the suggestions previously and hereinafter made with reference to your argument have equal application whether you are representing one party litigant or the other in the Appellate Court.

The law does not contemplate the making of objections in the Appellate Courts. If your adversary makes a misstatement of the facts, or in any manner gets out of the record, you cannot be heard to object. If you have a following argument you may at that time call the true situation to the attention of the Court. If not, you will just have to suffer in silence, and trust that the Court will discover the true facts when the record is read. This is one important respect in which argument in the Appellate Court differs from argument in the trial court.

In arguing the points of law to the Court you should not ordinarily read from law books. Your time is entirely too limited for such effort, and besides the Court will likely not appreciate this course of procedure. The Judges will feel that they can read the decisions for themselves and that you are unnecessarily taking up their time. It is best to state to the Court what the decisions hold, leaving to the Judges the reading of the cases, either as set forth in your brief or in the volumes themselves.

If there is some particular decision that you consider of such great importance to your case that it should be presented and read to the Court during your oral argument, you may do so, but in such event try and present only those parts and portions of the decision that are pertinent and read only such excerpts therefrom as are absolutely necessary.

When arguing a case in the Appellate Court you must be prepared to answer any questions about the case that the Judges may see fit to ask you. Of course, to meet this requirement you must be thoroughly familiar with the record in your case and fully prepared on the law. Some Appellate Court Judges ask many questions; some ask few. Having the Judges question you during your argument can sometime be quite disconcerting, but it is something that must be borne. If you have worked diligently on your case you should be able to answer any reasonable question that is asked. If you do not know the answer, do not guess at it. Tell the Court frankly that you do not know. There are no restrictions on the Appellate Court's right of interrogation and sometimes questions are asked by Judges which they could not answer themselves if they were in your place. Do not get the idea that the Judges are trying to embarrass you by their questions. They are merely seeking enlightenment in the case. The fact that they do ask questions usually indicates their interest. Bear in mind at all times that the Judges have no personal feeling in the matter, either with reference to you or your lawsuit. They are only attempting to arrive at a just decision.

Do not be fearful of the Appellate Courts. Though you find more dignity and ceremony in such courts than you do in the trial courts, always remember that the Judges are but human and differ little from other lawyers. As has been said by John W. Davis, once the Democratic nominee for the Presidency and a distinguished practitioner before the Supreme Court of the United States, "Courts of Appeal are not filled by demigods. Some members are learned, some less so. Some are keen and perspicacious, some have more plodding minds. In short they are [people] and lawyers much like the rest of us. That they are honest, impartial, ready and eager to reach a correct conclusion must always be taken for granted. You may rightfully expect and do expect nothing but fair treatment at their hands."[16]

In conclusion may it be said that if you will always prepare your case thoroughly, both in the trial courts and in the Appellate Courts, and present

---

[16] Francis L. Wellman, "Success in Court." By permission of The MacMillan Company, Publishers.

them in the manner best suited to your individual temperament and personality, and at all times to the very best of your ability, you will enjoy success in your profession. There are no short cuts. The road is a hard one of painstaking preparation and laborious performance, but the goal is worth the effort. Do your best – the angels can do no more.

THE END

INDEX